TUSKEGEE AIRMEN

JOHN PERRITANO

red rhino
bᴏᴏks®
NONFICTION

Area 51	Monsters on Land
Bioweapons	Mysterious Objects
Cannibal Animals	Racetracks
Cloning	The Science of Movies
Comet Catcher	Seven Wonders of the
Drones	Ancient World
Fault Lines	3D Printing
Gnarly Sports Injuries	Tiny Life
Great Spies of the World	**Tuskegee Airmen**
Hacked	Virtual Reality
Little Rock Nine	Wild Weather
Medal of Honor	Witchcraft
Military Dogs	Wormholes
Monsters of the Deep	Zombie Creatures

SADDLEBACK
EDUCATIONAL PUBLISHING
www.sdlback.com

Photo credits: page 12: Amoret Tanner/Alamy Stock Photo; page 13: Everett Collection Inc/Alamy Stock Photo; pages 24/25: Everett Collection Historical/Alamy Stock Photo; page 26: Everett Collection Inc/Alamy Stock Photo; pages 28/29: The Protected Art Archive/Alamy Stock Photo; pages 30/31: Everett Collection Historical/Alamy Stock Photo; page 32: Everett Collection Inc/Alamy Stock Photo; pages 34/35: Everett Collection Historical/Alamy Stock Photo; pages 36/37: PF-(aircraft)/Alamy Stock Photo; page 39: Stocktrek Images, Inc./Alamy Stock Photo; pages 40/41: Stocktrek Images, Inc./Alamy Stock Photo, page 46: Win McNamee/Getty Images News via Getty Images; page 48: Abaca Press/Alamy Stock Photo

ISBN: 978-1-68021-891-6
eBook: 978-1-64598-213-5

Printed in Malaysia
25 24 23 22 21   1 2 3 4 5

TABLE OF CONTENTS

Chapter 1
Red Tails...3

Chapter 2
War...8

Chapter 3
Black and White....................................14

Chapter 4
Learning to Fly.....................................20

Chapter 5
The 99th...24

Chapter 6
A New Base...27

Chapter 7
Waiting to Serve...................................33

Chapter 8
Call of Duty..38

Chapter 9
Winning Ways.......................................42

Chapter 10
Heroes..47

Glossary...50

Chapter 1
RED TAILS

It was 1944.

World War II was raging.

U.S. planes flew over Europe.

They had a job.

An oil field needed to be bombed.

This would hurt the enemy.

But there was a problem.

The planes were big.

They moved slowly.

Their engines were loud.

This made them easy targets.

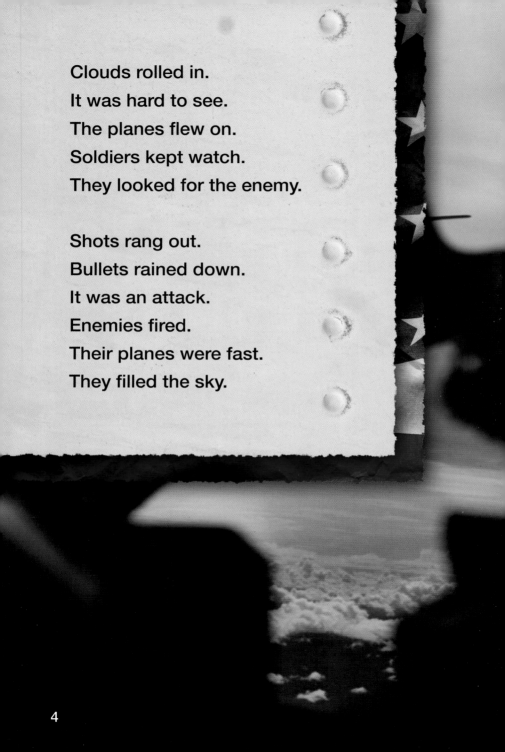

Clouds rolled in.
It was hard to see.
The planes flew on.
Soldiers kept watch.
They looked for the enemy.

Shots rang out.
Bullets rained down.
It was an attack.
Enemies fired.
Their planes were fast.
They filled the sky.

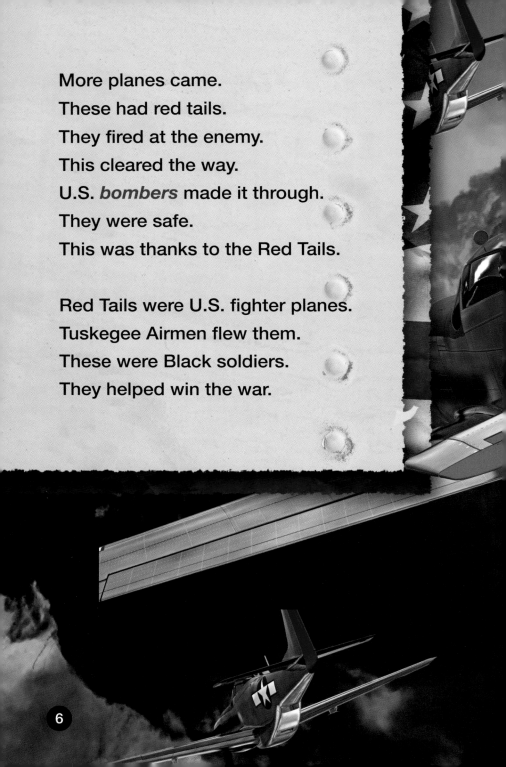

More planes came.

These had red tails.

They fired at the enemy.

This cleared the way.

U.S. *bombers* made it through.

They were safe.

This was thanks to the Red Tails.

Red Tails were U.S. fighter planes.

Tuskegee Airmen flew them.

These were Black soldiers.

They helped win the war.

HISTORY NOTE

P-51 Mustang

The P-51 was one of the best U.S. fighter planes. It could fly a long way and was a great attack plane.

Chapter 2

WAR

It was the 1930s.

Times were hard.

People in Europe *suffered*.

Many were out of work.

They had little to eat.

A man wanted to lead.

He made promises.

Many trusted him.

His power grew.

HISTORY NOTE

Benito Mussolini was the dictator of Italy from 1925 to 1945. He had close ties with Hitler during World War II.

The man became a *dictator*.

Adolf Hitler was his name.

He led Germany.

Other countries joined him.

His army grew.

Hitler knew people were down.

Their country had problems.

They wanted someone to blame.

He blamed a group of people.

Jews were the cause.

That is what he said.

Some believed him.

The leader made new laws.

Jews were taken away.

Officers put them in *prison camps*.

Many were killed.

But Hitler wanted more.

Power was one goal.

Getting land was another.

It was September 1, 1939.

He sent out his army.

World War II began.

The U.S. saw this.
They didn't support Hitler.
Still, no one wanted war.

A decision was made.
The U.S. would stay out of the war.
But they could not do this for long.

13

Chapter 3
BLACK AND WHITE

Racism is a big problem.
It is also part of U.S. history.

In the 1930s, people were *segregated*.
This was in the South.
Many states had rules.
These were based on race.
They were called Jim Crow laws.

The laws hurt Black people.

They could not be around whites.

There were separate schools.

White kids went to one.

Black kids had to go to another.

Bathrooms were separate too.

Some places only served white people.

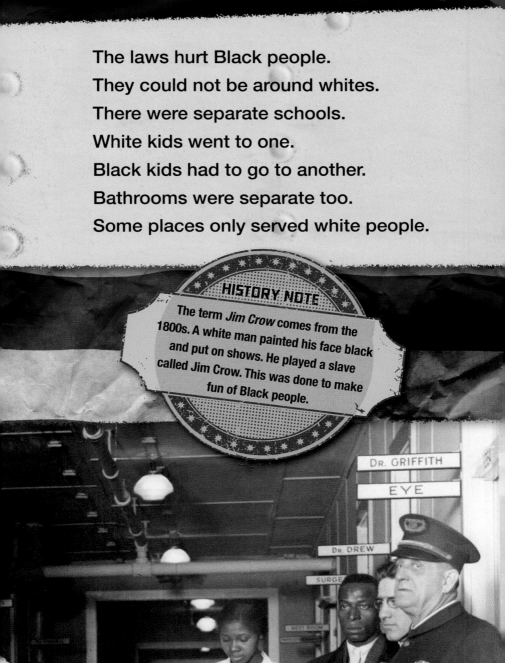

HISTORY NOTE

The term *Jim Crow* comes from the 1800s. A white man painted his face black and put on shows. He played a slave called Jim Crow. This was done to make fun of Black people.

DR. GRIFFITH

EYE

Dr. DREW

SURGE

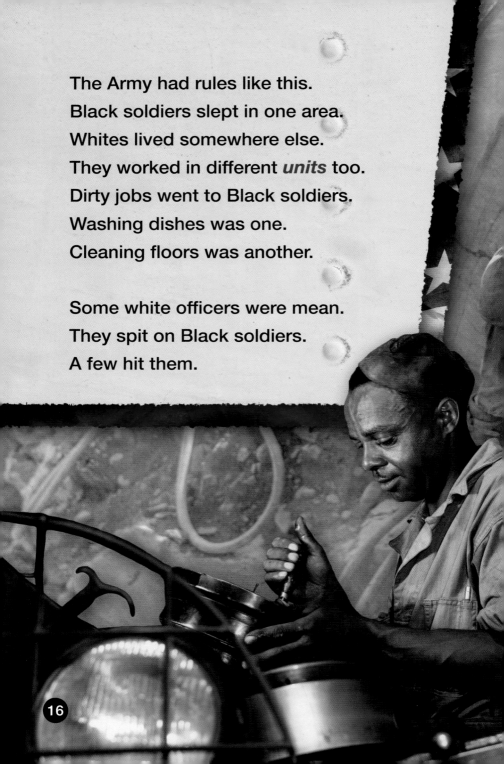

The Army had rules like this.
Black soldiers slept in one area.
Whites lived somewhere else.
They worked in different *units* too.
Dirty jobs went to Black soldiers.
Washing dishes was one.
Cleaning floors was another.

Some white officers were mean.
They spit on Black soldiers.
A few hit them.

Black soldiers did not give up.

The U.S. was their country too.

They wanted to fight for it.

Could some be pilots?

The Army said no.

But the war was growing fast.

Fighting got worse.

The U.S. had to be ready.

Help was needed.

Everyone had a part to play.

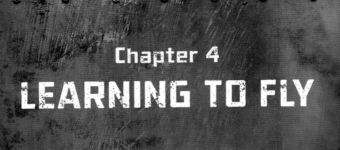

Chapter 4
LEARNING TO FLY

The war went on.

U.S. leaders got ready.

They might have to go to war.

More soldiers were needed.

Pilots were too.

Congress took action.

Flying schools were set up.

Civilians could learn to fly.

This included Black people.
But they could not train with whites.
Black people went to a special college.
It was called the Tuskegee Institute.
A Black man started the school.
His name was Booker T. Washington.

HISTORY NOTE

The Civilian Pilot Training Program trained 435,165 pilots from 1939 to 1944.

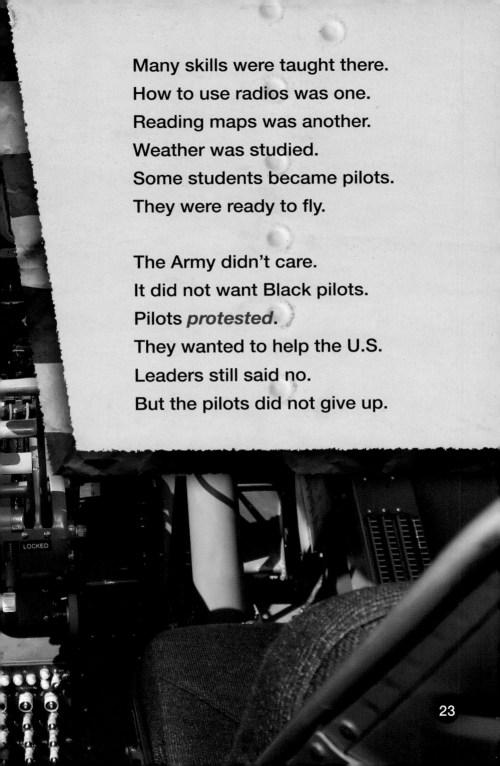

Many skills were taught there.

How to use radios was one.

Reading maps was another.

Weather was studied.

Some students became pilots.

They were ready to fly.

The Army didn't care.

It did not want Black pilots.

Pilots *protested*.

They wanted to help the U.S.

Leaders still said no.

But the pilots did not give up.

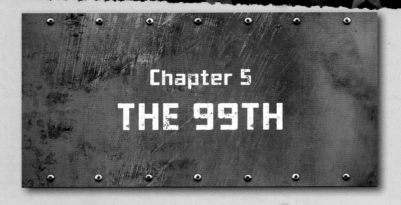

Chapter 5
THE 99TH

One Black pilot was *determined*.
His name was Yancey Williams.
He wanted to join the Army.
This was his dream.

Williams worked hard.

He passed all the tests.

But the Army still said no.

Then he took them to court.

It worked.

The Army did not want a trial.

They came up with a *solution*.

A new unit was set up.

It was the 99th Pursuit *Squadron*.

This was for Black pilots.

Williams soon joined.

HISTORY NOTE

Charles "Chief" Anderson taught himself to fly. He earned his pilot's license in 1929. In 1932, Anderson became the first African American pilot with a commercial license.

This was a big win.

Now Black soldiers had a shot.

First, they had to pass tests.

Then training began.

Finally they could be Army pilots.

Chapter 6
A NEW BASE

It was July 1941.

Tuskegee Army Air Base opened.

Many Black men signed up.

They wanted to train.

Some hoped to fly.

Others wanted to fix planes.

Their teachers were tough.

The men learned a lot.

HISTORY NOTE

P-40 Warhawk

The first P-40 could reach speeds of up to 300 miles per hour. The Tuskegee pilots flew these planes early in the war.

But life was not easy.

The men lived in tents.

They were treated badly.

Some white people didn't like them.

Many called them names.

29

A few white people reached out.
They wanted to help.
Eleanor Roosevelt was one.
She was the First Lady.
Roosevelt visited the school.
To get there, she took a plane.
It was flown by a Black man.

Why did she do this?
She wanted everyone to see.
Black people could fly planes.
Reporters were there.
They took photos.
The story was in the news.
It was a start.

The men kept training.
Some became officers.
Others went on to be pilots.
Many were crew members.
Now the men were ready to fight.
They could *defend* the U.S.

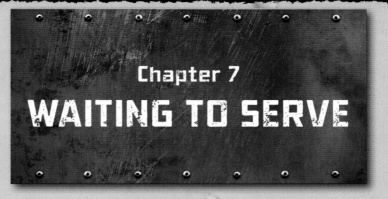

Chapter 7
WAITING TO SERVE

It was December 7, 1941.
The Japanese attacked.
They dropped bombs.
A U.S. Navy base was hit.
This was in Pearl Harbor, Hawaii.

Ships sank.
Planes blew up.
Fires burned.
Over 2,000 people died.
Most were sailors.

The U.S. made a decision.
They had to go to war.
There was no other choice.

It was March 7, 1942.

This was a big day at Tuskegee.

The first class of pilots got its wings.

Five men graduated.

They could now fly for the U.S.

A leader was chosen.

His name was Benjamin O. Davis Jr.

He went to an *elite* school.

This was the U.S. Military Academy.

Davis was the only Black *cadet* there.

Everyone else was white.

No one talked to him.

But he stayed.

Davis became an officer.

The Army chose him.

He would lead the 99th.

35

The men got ready.
White pilots went off to war.
Black pilots did not.
No one gave up.
They trained every day.

More Black men became pilots.
Additional units formed.
They waited.

The war got worse.
Then the 99th got the call.

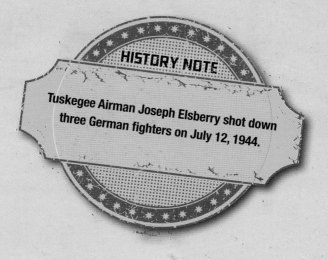

HISTORY NOTE

Tuskegee Airman Joseph Elsberry shot down three German fighters on July 12, 1944.

Chapter 8
CALL OF DUTY

The 99th went to war.

This was on April 15, 1943.

They were sent to North Africa.

Davis led them into battle.

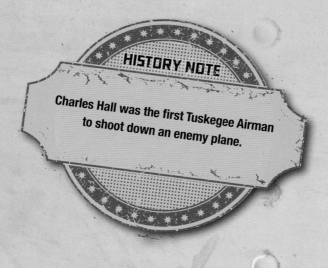

HISTORY NOTE

Charles Hall was the first Tuskegee Airman to shoot down an enemy plane.

It was June 6, 1943.

Four Black pilots made history.

They were the first to fight.

The men flew into battle.

Enemies fired at them.

The 99th fought back.

All came home safe.

Their next job was hard too.
U.S. bombers flew.
These were big planes.
They moved slowly.
Protection was needed.

The 99th had fast planes.
They flew next to the bombers.
Their tails were painted red.
Bomber crews could see them.
It made them feel safe.

"Red Tails" became their nickname.
They were good at their jobs.
Bomber crews gave them another name.
It was "Red Tail Angels."

HISTORY NOTE

P-47 Thunderbolt

Nicknamed the "Jug," the P-47 flew higher than most fighter planes. Tuskegee pilots started flying the Thunderbolt in June 1944.

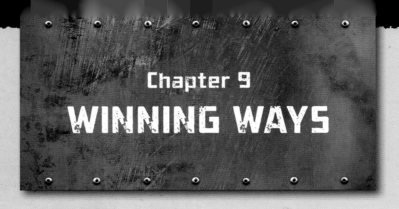

Chapter 9
WINNING WAYS

It was 1944.

There was a big attack.

This happened in Italy.

German planes shot at ships.

The 99th gave chase.

It was a tough fight.

Ten enemy planes were shot down.

The Red Tails got three more the next day.

They were heroes.

The pilots got an award.

People saw how good they were.

World War II went on.

The Airmen flew strong.

They were always on the go.

Sometimes the men flew with other units.

White pilots saw them in action.

One thing was clear.

The 99th could fly.

They fought smart too.

One mission turned bad.

Many units were sent out.

The 99th was one of them.

Thousands of fliers were lost.

Some were killed.

Others got *captured*.

Not one was a Tuskegee pilot.

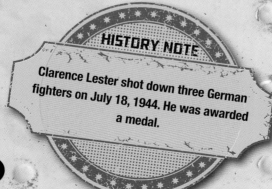

HISTORY NOTE

Clarence Lester shot down three German fighters on July 18, 1944. He was awarded a medal.

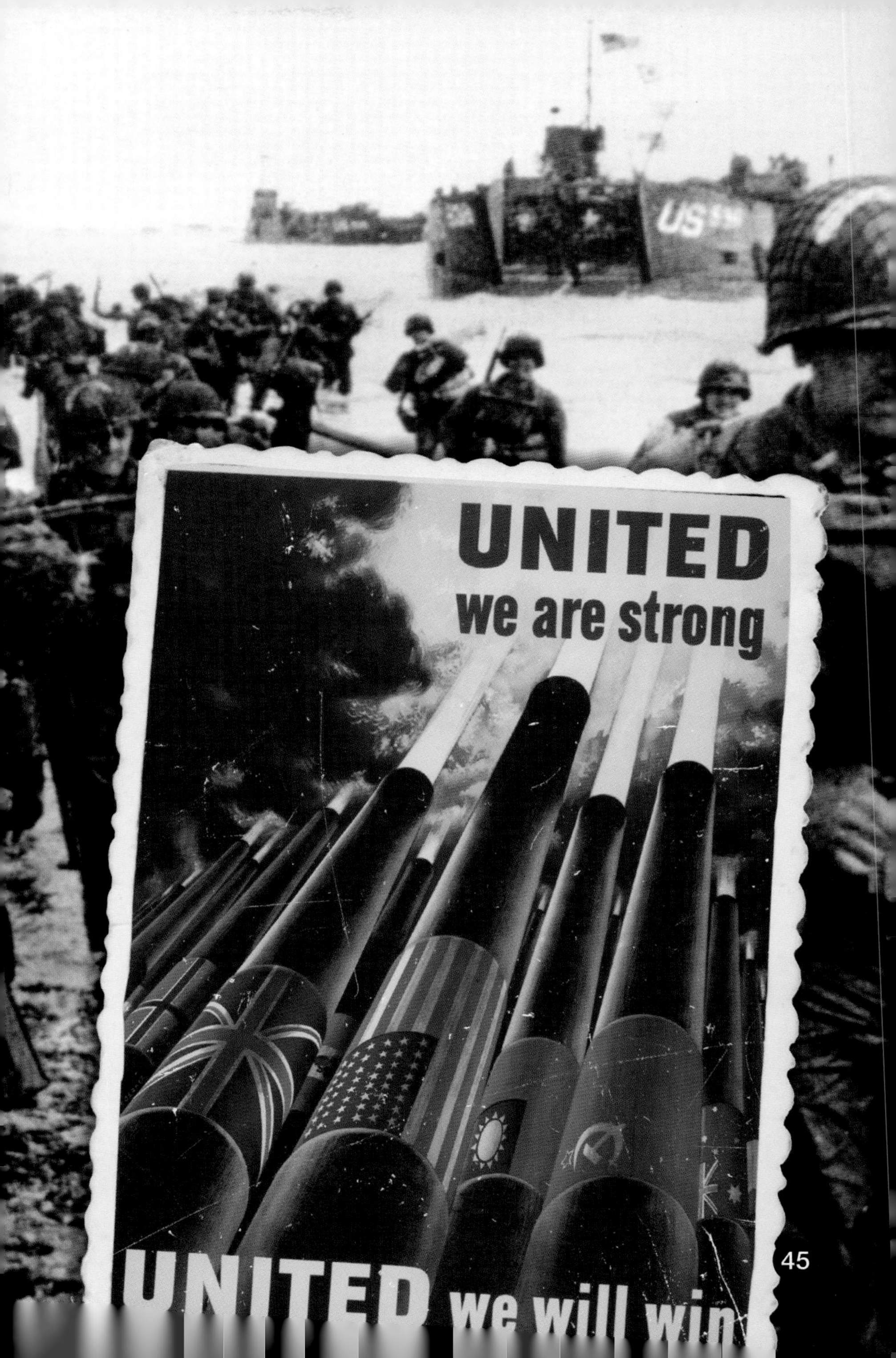
US
UNITED
we are strong
UNITED we will win

The Red Tails flew many missions.

They shot down 112 enemy planes.

Even one enemy ship was hit.

Sixty-six Airmen died in the war.

Thirty-two became *POWs*.

They got many medals.

Their *bravery* saved lives.

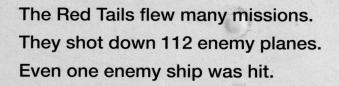

HISTORY NOTE

James Walker was shot down over Yugoslavia on July 22, 1944. He survived and traveled 300 miles to safety.

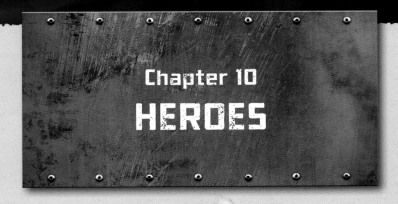

Chapter 10
HEROES

World War II ended in 1945.

The Airmen went home.

Not much had changed.

The U.S. was still divided.

Black people were not equal.

But the pilots remained strong.

Some stayed in the military.

Others did not.

A few wanted to fly jets.

They were not hired.

Things did change.

But it took time.

President Truman helped.

Truman knew about the Airmen.
He liked what they did.
The president ordered changes.
Black soldiers were no longer kept separate.
They could train with whites.

The pilots were proud.
They had done their part.
Their work helped win the war.
It also opened doors.
Minds were changed.
People saw them in a new way.
There was still work to do.
But change was coming.
Black people would get more *rights*.

People still talk about the Airmen.
Congress gave them a medal.
This was in 2006.
It was a big *honor*.

Two years later, something big happened.
A Black man became president.
He was the first.
His name was Barack Obama.

President Obama honored the Airmen too.
They were there when he was sworn in.
The president called them heroes.
His message was clear.
These men made his success possible.

GLOSSARY

bomber: a plane made for dropping bombs

bravery: bold or fearless actions

cadet: a student training to be a military officer

capture: to take someone prisoner

civilian: a person not in the military

Congress: part of the U.S. government; the House of Representatives and the Senate

defend: to fight to keep or protect something

determined: committed to doing something

dictator: a ruler with complete control over a country

elite: part of a high-level group

honor: respect and recognition for a person

POW: stands for prisoner of war; a soldier captured by an enemy during battle

prison camp: a place where prisoners are kept during war

protest: to object to something in an organized way

rights: privileges that belong to people and are protected by the law

segregate: to separate people by race

solution: an answer to a problem

squadron: a military unit made up of planes and their crews

suffer: to experience pain or unpleasantness

unit: a small military group led by an officer

CLONING

DO YOU COPY?

Dolly was named after singer Dolly Parton.

A sheep is a living animal.
How can it be copied?
It is not easy.
Doctors work with *cells*.
They take *genes* out of one cell.
They put them in a new one.

Things can go wrong.
It took a long time to make Dolly.
277 tries.
She was the first cloned *mammal*.

Most sheep live for 10 years.
Dolly lived only six.
But she was a success.
She made big news.
Cloning took off after that.

4

5

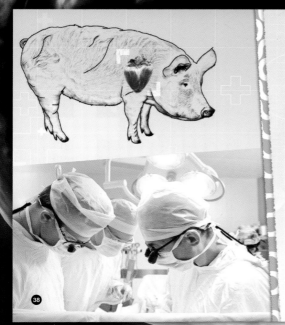

Cloning can do more.
Some people need new organs.
They need a *transplant*.
There are not enough.
People wait a long time.
Many die.

Some doctors had an idea.
They tried pig organs.
Pig organs are like ours.
Doctors put them into people.
But they were rejected.
Human bodies did not like them.

What if the organs had human genes?
They would act like human organs.
They might not be rejected.
Doctors want to find out.

Chapter 9
SHOULD WE CLONE?

The science is exciting.
It can help the sick.
Doctors learn from it.
Find cures.
Save lives.
But it is still a gamble.
We do not know a lot.

Cloning can have big risks.
Stem cells look like *cancer* cells.
They can act the same too.
Divide a stem cell.
Do it over and over.
The cells may turn into cancer cells.
That is what some think.

NONFICTION

9781680210316

9781680210729

9781680218787

9781680218886

9781680210477

9781680218626

9781680210538

9781680210712

9781680218893

9781680218770

9781680210552

9781680210545

WWW.REDRHINOBOOKS.COM
MORE TITLES COMING SOON

9781680210750

9781680210286

9781680218633

9781680210781

9781680210767

9781680210507

9781680218909

9781680210736

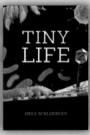

9781680210774

9781680218916

9781680210361

9781680210514

9781680210323

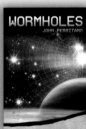

9781680210330

9781680210743